www.mattheweaglin.com

Interior & Cover Design
The Reel Return, LLC | Chicago, IL
www.thereelreturn.com

ISBN: 978-0-578-54136-5

Published in the United States of America

*The author and respective parties are neither financial coaches nor certified accountants of any means. The principles, concepts, and tips discussed in this book are a result of the author's own personal money management and acquired knowledge through lived experience, research, and mentoring from affluent figures in his life. The REEL RETURN, LLC, as the publisher, and the author are not responsible for guaranteed results or any losses for any individual.

Proactive Practice

Becoming Less Reactive To Become More Proactive In Everyday Financial Management

Opening Remarks

Let's GO! Welcome to anew. A brighter day is coming for your financial management and it starts with this book, planner, and digital budget analyzer. It is long time for the days of living paycheck-to-paycheck to end. It is long time for the days of living without ends meet to come to a close. It is long time for you to live the life you want and have the necessary finances to do so. If you cannot commit to yourself to mature in your financial discipline, this book is not for you. However, if you are ready to go the mile for **you**, I am ready to run with you!

Growing up in a single parent home, I saw my mother struggle between the choice of keeping a roof over my head or having time for nurturing, leisure, and self-care. I made a choice very early in life that I did not want my mom to purchase my wants, and like that, as a result of my decisiveness, every skill I have ever developed has transformed into a stream of revenue.

I started my entrepreneurial journey at 10-years-old after she taught me how to mow the yard. I saw how she started her business, and I wanted to start my own too! From that one stream of income, I learned that if I needed to invest in myself to learn another skill, I could earn the funds to invest in my own study. Since then, the sky has been the limit in the number of hours I study investing in my own craft and building my skill set. Not to mention, as more money has come into the pot, the more responsible I needed to become. It was so different because financial management, budgets, and other things that we must monitor in our financial journey comes so natural for me.

As I reflect to lead you on this journey, the first place to get started in reshaping our financial management or mismanagement is in the mind. Why the mind, you ask? The mind holds the values that are created from our youth; the mind holds how we perceive money and transaction, which drives the habits, thus, affecting the items we buy, subscribe, and devote massive funds to live over budget but with the sting of debt burying us in a place of seemingly no return. Like any habit, though, our learned spending habits can be changed.

Matthew chapter seven verse 14 describes just how disciplined we must be to achieve the life that most people will not attain. " For the gate is narrow and the way is hard that leads to life, and those who find it are few".

Your most valuable assets are time, energy, and the thirst for knowledge. We must be very cautious to do activities that contribute to our legacy. Time reverses for no one.

Too many people grow comfortable in their circumstance whether it's working a job to keep bills paid or building a career from someone else offering an opportunity that they can snatch from you at *any time*.

You have to make a choice. There needs to be a major paradigm shift, especially if you've been raised in an impoverished community. Poverty is a state of mind. It spreads just as worse as a wildfire. To be broke is to live life from a broken spirit. The ultimate difference is that many of us are overcoming a cash flow problem in the words of Les Brown, but when we exist in these severe spaces, this can trigger a heart that has no hope. Be of good courage, my friend.

Are you ready for change? Once you make the choice to be proactive in your finances and choose to develop the gift inside of you, ideas, money, and other opportunities will start coming to you. No matter how your bank account looks at the current circumstance…know that your gift will always make room for you.

I made the choice nearly 14-years-ago and since that day, I have notes on top of notes, mentors in every area that I want to invest my time, and opportunity has become present around nearly every corner I turn.

As I mentioned earlier, our values are established in our youth, so let's take it back to the basics. My mom and her mother taught me the value of a principle. I guess they knew, from there, I'd figure it out and that God would expose me to different environments and situations, but I needed to understand the value of certain key principles.

Every principle must deliver a promise. No matter what –if you follow the principle to the letter, it must fulfill the promise that is tied to it.

Contents

Discipline Is Strength

The first thing that needs to change in order for us to truly commit to becoming financially secure is to transform our perspective on how we understand discipline according to our dream. To serve people… to find a solution or make an impact that the world needs, then and only then will bring great reward. Think about all of the greats. You have your Kobe Bryant, Michael Jackson, Jay-z, Bill Gates, The Beatles, Oprah… the list goes on. What do or did they believe they can do in their lifetime? Is it any different than your dreams? I have so many youth in the programs I've taught say, "I want to be one of the greatest basketball players [or rappers] that ever lived," when I ask them about their dreams. The most limiting thing for many of us is to put our profit in front of the people we serve.

Generating revenue will never be an issue once you walk in the gift you've been given. We resonate and want to resemble the stars we see in sports, entertainment, and other industries. What do these people do that is different than all the rest? They changed their idea about **DISCIPLINE** and giving back to their community. The first part of the word looks like what? The answer is disciple. Oprah… Will Smith… Tyler Perry… they all became disciples of their craft. The battle starts in the mind. If we are looking to become like some of those greats we should channel all of our energy to become disciples of our industry, practice, and concepts. Are you going to choose to get out of bed at 6 A.M. and start your day working for yourself or get ready 30-60 minutes before you have to go work for someone else? What will you do to secure your own future every morning, noon, or evening? The second part of this is are you willing to give away your gift for free until others find the value you have to add to their lives? Notice that I did not say recognize. The world is looking for answers that are in each and every one of us. It is the gift! All of those people above have made an impact through their natural gift whether it was through television, the radio, texts, or the Internet. They leveraged their impact through different mediums to be found.

I'd be remiss if I did not have a transparent moment…

Trust me! I was not always as structured, and I certainly did not exercise these beliefs that are talked about in this book. As I grow older, I am becoming more consistent in my discipline with my craft, and I recognize that all quality things must take time to develop, even our ideas and value system.

Here's how.

My complicated relationship with discipline arose early on. Let's just say I remember so many instances where I received chastisement in my youth for not doing the right thing, not cleaning my room, acting out in school, embarrassing my family… you name it. Half the time it wasn't even my family members doing the hitting. As a result, I subconsciously paired discipline with punishment.

It wasn't until the day I decided to try something new as far as staying disciplined in my studies that I realized discipline is not punishment; it is making the utilization of the principle regularly to develop unconscious behavior that breeds grounds for great reward. Notice that I did not say gives guaranteed results. Even with discipline, you and I might not always win, but at least when we fail, identifying the area of struggle is eased being able to use the lens of our training.

After growing in my understanding I had to change the way I processed my life. You can grow stagnant without the proper daily mental stimulation, faith, and affirmations. Know that your gift, the discipline that you put in… it will work!

I learned to stay positive even in the midst of calamity. I never understood how to stay focused on positive thinking, but now, I understand that I must be inspired, motivated, and reminisce about blessings from the other challenges I've faced and incorporate other people's stories into my repertoire of faith...

The most significant of these, though, is to believe in your craft. The life of an entrepreneur is very lonely. Something that has really kept me is creating a playlist of inspirational speakers on Youtube that I listen to every morning. There is so much negativity around every corner, but if you focus on what you believe, populating your mind with motivation from people who are where you want to be, you will have the energy to push further in your studies for your craft.

Learn how to train your mind to think differently on how to solve any issue. One of the greatest lines I've heard in my lifetime was to "imagine the possibilities". Imagine the possibilities if you could be the only one in the room with an answer. Imagine if you pushed harder, studied longer, applied your craft just as hard as you study it, then when it came time to attack an issue, because you've trained your mind to not think regularly, it won't respond like the average person –defeated. The other word on the side of discipline is that there will come moments of defeat. Defeat is only associated with an isolated event, although we love to tie it with our life's work. With an unorthodox approach to problem solving, you'll even be able to defeat the idea and feelings of being defeated.

Most importantly though, train your mind to have a rest mode –even the greatest entrepreneur can fry his brain. Mobile technology has a sleep mode for crying out loud. As we pursue our craft, our ambition can drive us mad. Please know that your rest is the key to you having the brain power to solve issues and to welcome inspiration. Ever tried to inspire a crowd of tired people? It's nearly impossible. Please rest.

All of these things I've learned have only been a benefit to me in my journey. I study hard, and I apply. Trust me receiving "No" as I attempt to make a sale is way worse than understanding the concept that I must encounter more "No" responses than "Yes" to find my audience.

Needless to say, if you train your mind to openly accept the discipline needed to excel in your craft, you will stand out. The mind communicates to the body what to do, how to respond, and to achieve it, by any means necessary. Take those baby steps. To change the trajectory of your family, you have to make the conscience choice to do something different. Dr. King said, "If you can't fly then run, if you can't run then walk, if you can't walk then crawl, but whatever you do you have to keep moving forward".

Bringing The Pennies Home

The main thing I remember learning from both my mother and grandmother is no matter how small the value, it is still of value and can add value to you. That has stuck with me to this day! I see so many people walk past one-cent on the street, in restaurants, malls… everywhere. When I started my savings account, I remember I saved so many pennies and other small coins that my first deposit was nearly $300 because I would find or save pennies, nickels, and dimes since I was three-years-old. ***Everything holds value even if it's at the lowest value.*** In our currency, the penny is the lowest value to give for transaction purposes.

To give you a better example, if you were to average out a work life at 45-years and say you saved one-dollar every day, you would have nearly $17,000 dollars saved for emergency, leisure, or to add to your retirement fund.

Let's scale this up for business owners. Think about it…if you add up every straw paper that is produced for an entire country and according to a CNN article by Jacqueline Howard, on October 3, 2018, "On any given day in the United States, an estimated 36.6% or approximately 84.8 million adults consume fast food," said Cheryl Fryar in the article. It's time to do the math. What's the revenue generated from those straw sales assuming there is one-person per order (the lowest value)? The straw paper company would reap nearly $850,000 "on any given day", assuming the straw paper costs one cent. Who would've even thought that you needed to dress a straw with paper, right? But, someone did think of it, and I wonder how comfortable they're living their life at the moment.

No Limits, No Problem

After changing the way you process discipline and understanding the value of money, to put everything in perspective, you must utilize a budget. A budget is just that; it should keep you from budging over the limits you set for yourself to move towards your goals. Because money is needed to gain more in this life, how would you want to spend your money? Do you want to make sure your month's bills are covered, food, transportation, etc? Do you want to make purchases now and not have a nice savings account, reserve funds, or attractive retirement fund?

With a budget, you can take into account the monies you need for bills, necessities, and even yourself. It's a see before I touch type of thing.

Every dime you get from work should not go towards your living style. You don't have to purchase food every time friends are going out. Have you tried eating at home and going to socialize instead of buying food that is very generously over-priced and may not even fulfill?

Creating a budget can be done on loose leaf paper when you're a child, but as I've grown, I utilize Microsoft Excel to guarantee my numbers are right; I can run different hypotheticals –the "what ifs" of me spending this money.

The first thing you want to be sure of is that your rent/ mortgage, water, gas, and heat bills are resolved. This should not exceed more than 35-percent of your income. God forbid something were to happen where you only went to work for one pay period and received one full check out of the month. You would still have a roof over your head and able to have lights, cooking capabilities, heat, and a hot shower to enjoy.

The second thing you want to cover is your transportation to arrive on-time for work to make the money. This should not exceed more than 15-percent of your income. Why 15-percent? Every month you may have a car note, service, maintenance, and gas designated for work purposes only. For those carpooling, using public transportation, or other modes, there is more than likely a monthly fee associated, which far exceeds the cost of a seven-day pass. You may need to throw in an umbrella, poncho, snow boots, hand warmers, etc. if you are using public transportation.

For those who have a vehicle, no matter how new the car is…you should save for a rainy day. Car repairs can cost well over the amount of an oil change, and you really don't want to have to wait for another check to come in to pay for those repairs. Let alone, how would you get to work if your car is in the shop? Those funds should be more than sufficient, over time, to cover those expenses. Everything, eventually, needs repairs…our own bodies need fixing in due time for crying out loud!

The third category is your mediums of communication, which is five-percent of your income. Your phone bill, internet, and cable should not exceed more than five percent because you can actually utilize one main device for unlimited internet access/ streaming capabilities, and other than that, you only need basic cable where you can access at minimum news outlets and educational shows. Mostly everything is accessible over the internet now. I am not saying you can't have a TV, but when it comes to multiple bills and you already have one device with one bill that is capable to gain access to the world wide web, tether, receive calls, Google anything, and has HDMI compatibility, why give away money?

The next category is very important. You need to have your insurance policies (5%). This means you should have home, auto, and life insurance policies. You never know when you may have an accident whether it is your fault or not, but it may even be fatal. Do not leave your family without any help to fulfill different costs once you are gone.

The fifth category is your savings. This should not exceed over 15-percent of your income. Charity, general savings, emergency fund, and your retirement contributions should all be included within this fifteen percent. You can allocate ten-percent of your funds to a non-profit for something we will discuss later about paying it forward. Every year you want to lookup things about the tax code with charitable donations. Search it in Google and see if you are eligible for adding it as a deduction on your taxes next year. All of the other subcategories following like your emergency fund can be allocated according to your needs.

The sixth is your play money feel free to allocate 15-percent of your income here as well. You work hard for your money, and you need some funds to enjoy leisure, family time, a new outfit, or what have you. The food in this category is also for groceries; this expense changes per month depending upon your leisure activities.

Lastly, the seventh category is for financing (*10%). This ten-percent can be allocated to any of the above categories if you do not have any creditor-monitored commitments, but if you do, put forth the effort to never allow your minimum payments on credit cards, student loan payments, collections exceed this ten-percent mark referenced from your monthly income. We will discuss credit more in the chapters ahead.

The final thing you want to be sure of is that you know exactly the base amount of what is needed in each account or your goal that ensures at the beginning of each month x-amount of dollars should be in my account. This is all dependent upon the time check #1 and check #2 are received, corresponding with bill-check allocation. Doing this will keep away those ugly overdraft fees.

Law Of Transaction

The most vital understanding of currency is that it must cycle whether that is from business-to-customer and back or between your own financial economy –all of your checking and savings accounts. A healthy cycle is beneficial to the economy and your own pockets. The ease-of access cycle between your checking accounts should be established. Accounts that feature Zelle are, in my experience, the best to open. It allows you to not only send money to your accounts, but you can also receive funds as well almost immediately without paying fees for transfers.

"This note is legal tender for all debts, public and private," is printed on every bill produced by the Federal Reserve.

When you are hired, the company owes you a debt for the amount of time worked. You, then, are obligated to pay yourself, your lenders that provide you living essentials (mortgage, gas, electricity), and everything else on your budget sheet. These monthly obligations will grow tiresome if you only have one source of income. This is also outside of the fact that your job could lay you off and you never see it coming.

Imagine your income sources as different streams that flow into a huge body of water. If one pool in that stream or the stream itself is blocked how full and or clear will the body of water be?

Multiple streams of income are the saving grace of having a job that has the power to give you your pink slip at any time. These other streams could be another part time job as a supplement, a hustle as direct income, and other passive income. You could even have several sources of passive income.

The goal is to become financially stable. Stability comes when you are able to manipulate the funds you receive, earn or receive multiple checks, and have all of your responsibilities paid. This is the law of transaction exercised in your personal finances. For every debt earned, debt is paid. There is no such thing as financial freedom.

Now, the secret that ties into the transactions is the difference between the pain you feel when you spend.

So often we find ourselves living above our means. We

love to drive the fanciest and newest cars, get the biggest house on the block, or go out nearly every weekend and spend astronomical amounts of money. How the heck does this happen? Not having the posture to accept delayed gratification is one piece of the puzzle, but studies have proven that the one or several pieces of plastic in our wallets **do not** register the amount of pain as if we were to hand over the funds needed to pay for some of these transactions in cash. We are so used to being only a swipe away from getting what we want either with a debit or credit card, and this cycle is not healthy at all.

Building Credit, Builds Rapport

Some people fear credit. Others use credit to their benefit. Which are you?

Credit is borrowing money from a lender. Plain and simple. Credit reports are the details of your entire history with each lender you borrowed from and your management in an effort to pay those funds back. From this, a score is given to you based on criteria set by Experian, Transunion, and Equifax. So yes, student loans, mortgages, rent and other accounts opened in your name will reflect on your report.

As it relates to your initial credit card and/ or credit line, are you worth a $5,000 credit limit based off of your income and credit history? Creditors will give you a shot and usually start you with a low credit limit when you are approved for your first card. This limit says that you cannot use more than the say $5,000 from the above scenario. However, there is a system to the game. You never want to spend above 30-percent of this amount. This will start to "nip" away at your credit score. Though, you also want to be reasonable in how you use the card to build your payment history.

After you use the card, there will be a minimum payment that you are responsible to pay, but here's the trick...don't pay the minimum. You always want to give more to show that you "appreciate" the lending you received and within a certain time. The Bible talks about giving credit to where credit is due. You want to show them that you are committed to paying off what you borrowed; however, you want to do this over time to boost your credit score, and in turn, your creditors will increase your credit limit. The best way to think about this is to think that the higher my denominator is the more (but I don't suggest) you could spend. So If I have a $30,000 credit limit, how much can I spend without having severe penalties toward my score? The answer is $9,000. If I have a $100,000 total credit limit, what can I spend?

The type of accounts for your lines of credit, average age of all of your accounts, and hard inquiries matter as well.

Credit Factors

Hard Inquiries 10% 55 points	Account Diversity 10% 55 points	Credit Age 15% 82.5 points	Amount Owed 30% 165 points	Payment History 35% 192.5 points

One of the best things I've come across in this day and age is using services offered by retail stores to where I don't have to get a ding on my credit report, but I can still purchase what I need with or without an interest rate. They connect to your bank accounts and allow you monthly or bi-weekly payments. These apps, literally, will not let you connect a credit card to protect your current debt. If that's not integrity, I don't know what is.

Never buy what you cannot payback in the amount of time that it is owed back. You should get cards that give points and cashback. This will benefit you. Also, search and find the companies with the best promotions. You want to find the cards that have the longest 0% APR (annual percentage rate), but you want to make sure that by the time the APR promotion is over, the card is paid off. A credit card is a form of unsecured debt. This type of debt is paired with every type of high interest rate.

Building your credit earlier than most can give you a major gain when it comes to other secured debt that you may need such as purchasing a house, car, or any other major purchase you need to use borrowed funds to complete.

Tips:

1. Pay down balance and remain less than or equal to 30%
2. Diversify accounts
3. Start building your credit ASAP
4. Add key dates in your calendar about when promotions end, balance rectification checkpoints, and payment dates
5. Link your debit account for financing monthly payments with each financing account
6. Pay within the 25-day statement balance and try to pay another time before or on your due date to quickly decrease the balance

Pay It Forward

The best blessings I've seen are when I am blessing the lives of others, and they are prospering from either the dollar, time, or wisdom I was able to give. There are so many different forms a return on investment could be delivered to you in your time of need or just as another blessing.

When you tithe, give to others, and doing all of it without expectation of receiving anything –except for maybe a thank you— you are creating your own bank of blessings to return to you. We are all human. We all have bad times at one point or another. When you take the time to care for someone else, you will reap what you've sown, and I'm sorry to say this but it won't be in monetary form all of the time. However, your need will be supplied.

Let's talk about when you sacrifice now to still pay it forward. Yes, there are levels to this giving thing. My mother left six figures and "pretty much made a vow of poverty" she says. The generational blessings passed down to my sister and I that we've been able to reap were from her sacrifices. It gets so deep to the point of even those coming after you will be blessed. That's what you call post-generational blessings!

Your Most Valuable Assets

You must budget your most valuable assets: time, energy, and knowledge. These are the utmost essentials if you are really wanting to stay committed to the goals you set and the dream you want to fulfill.

Your energy is very dispensable and lucrative for other people's lives. Set aside time for yourself, family, and lastly your job. I find it so often that people allow their day job to consume every ounce of life inside of them to the point that they cannot function except to make dinner and drop in the bed to wake up and do the exact same thing all over again the next day. This may sound cliché, but so many people have done this throughout much of life, and they've died not having their gifts fully manifest.

Set aside time to learn, to inspire, and to purge.

Just because you have a gift does not mean that you

know everything. There are others with a similar gifting, but their caliber may be different if they're further in their mission than you are at the moment.

Time is the one thing you will never get back. Do things right when you learn about it to truly benefit. You cannot reset the clock on a retirement fund. Many people wish they could. Know that many people will come to use all of your time.

Walk Through The Open Door

Everyone has a gift inside of them. It is your job to nurture the grounds for that specific talent to blossom. Take the time to learn about you. Although you may work a nine-to-five right now, you have what it takes to be your own boss. Might I remind you though, your day job can and will condition you into a complacency zone that will trap the gift inside of you.

There are still to this day so many who condition themselves out of what is inside of them because of what their environment says, family, and even their own self-doubt. I say to you though start putting it to work. Give your gift a chance and see what happens. You'll begin to notice opportunity, ideas, and a peace will begin to manifest.

Using the gift inside of you will open door after door after door for you to begin to prosper. Don't look at the gift as a prosperity tool but use it in a way that your perspective should be how can I use this gift to help others. After enough people see that you can help them solve their issues, you'll begin a vast current of money through your accounts. Don't settle. Gifts are oftentimes hard to open, but what's inside is always well-worth the wait.

About The Author

Matthew Eaglin-Daniels is an American entrepreneur, author, and success coach. He is a fanatic for self-improvement and a higher understanding. His life has been marked with pursuing knowledge and wisdom to share with so many that need to see hope and learn a new way.

Eaglin-Daniels is the President & CEO of The Reel Return. Being in its youthful years, the company focuses on delivering digital media and marketing services for individuals and business owners nationwide, however, based in Chicago, IL.

He is a graduate of The University of Illinois at Urbana-Champaign where he studied broadcast journalism. Eaglin-Daniels excels in storytelling and has been able to communicate his story through his natural gift.

His unique encounters and experiences tied with his age gives him a very relatable edge for youth and adults alike.

He's served his community alongside his mother on the south side of Chicago for the past 15-years as she has dedicated her life's work to youth and their families through IMPACT Family Center.

He's seen how the absence of a father can severely deter youth from tapping into their full potential and purpose. He's seen the devastating effects of financial illiteracy take tolls on generations of black and brown people. He's seen the damaging tales of toxic relationships, dysfunctional families, and a torn people.

Through these three texts he's written, he plans to not only share his message, but lead workshops to help others become the masters of their life financially, relationally, and spiritually.

Also Available

Made in United States
North Haven, CT
04 November 2026

21733840R00029